MW01631287

GEORGE'S ENERGY ADVENTURE

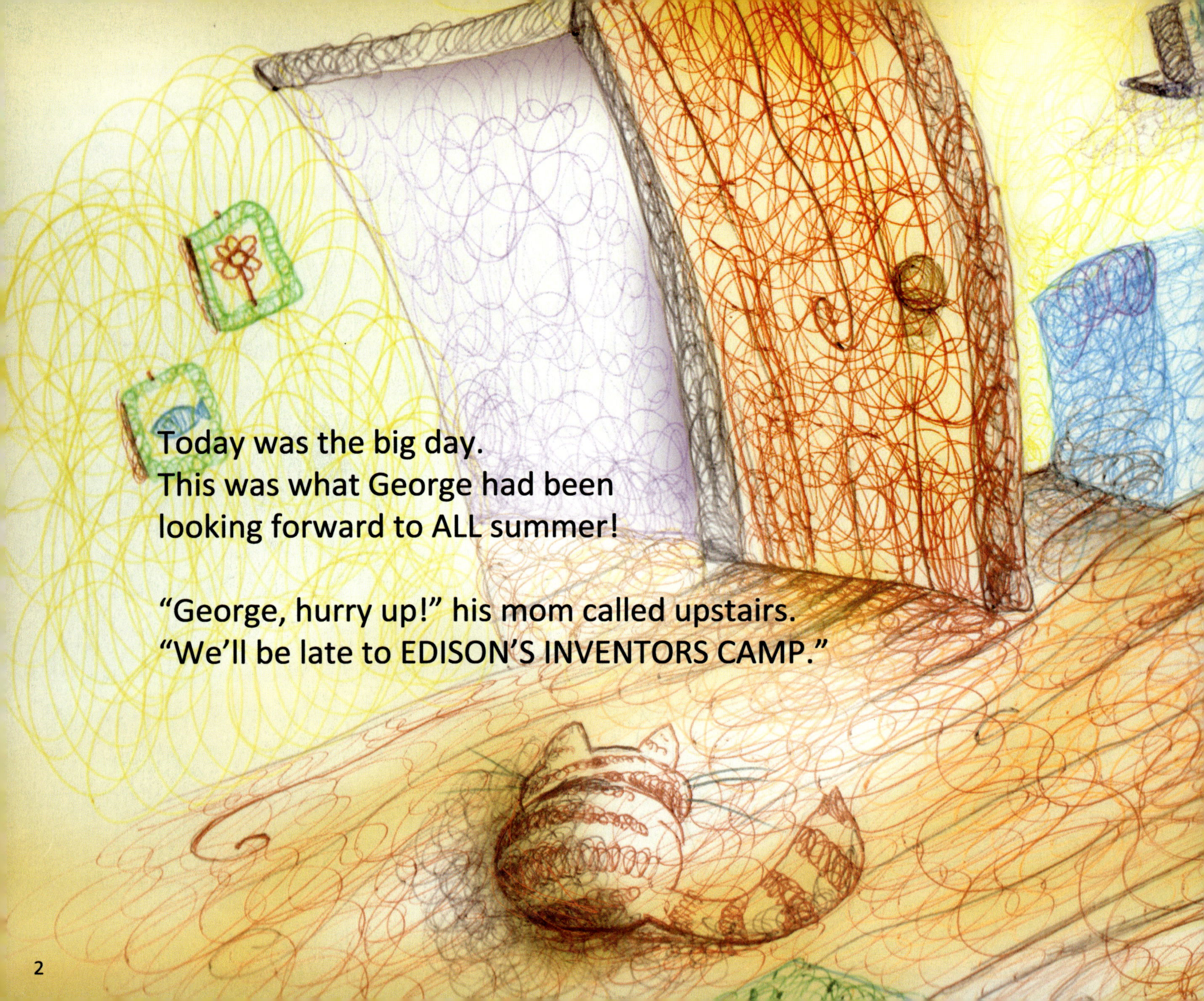

Today was the big day.
This was what George had been
looking forward to ALL summer!

“George, hurry up!” his mom called upstairs.
“We’ll be late to EDISON’S INVENTORS CAMP.”

Nothing could be better than hanging out with friends while learning about science. This year they were exploring energy.

"Hello, inventors! I'm Ms. Megawatt."
"Mega-what?" said the girl next to George.
"Mega-WATT," said the camp leader.
"I'm a bundle of energy
in a short amount of time!
Let's get going!"

"This year your project is something you will ALL love! You are going to build your own city! But, you must keep the lights on by using what you learned about energy."

The girl next to George jumped out of her seat in excitement and said, “I know a kind of energy that runs all the time no matter what the weather is like!”

"Don't short circuit, Marie,"
said Ms. Megawatt,
"Cool down and listen"

“You will be using building blocks to make a city where YOUR children will live someday,” Ms. Megawatt explained.

The children giggled with glee. "Remember that all cities need energy. They need a lot of energy! They need it all the time—every hour, every day."

George knew exactly what to do. He began to build.
“Do you want to work as a team?” Marie asked.
“No. I’m already going to make the best city ever.
I don’t need your help,” said George.

"Are you using nuclear energy?
I learned that it's great for big cities!"
Marie exclaimed happily.

"Who needs nuclear energy?"
George said impatiently.
"My parents have solar panels
on our house.
That is all anyone needs."

Block after block, George added houses, stores, and solar panels.
He soon ran out of blocks for all the solar panels he needed for his city. Cities need A LOT of energy!

George was stuck. He tried and tried.
He could not build enough energy for
his city. Frustrated, he knocked
his city down and stormed off to bed.

George opened his eyes and saw a strange city.
"Wait, I know this city. It's mine!"
Looking up and down, and all around, George heard a warm, friendly voice.

"Hi George, my name is Sunny. I heard you created this city! Come meet everyone that keeps this place running."

Curiously, George followed Sunny into the familiar city. As clouds began to drift across the sky, Sunny slowed to a stop.

“I’m sorry. I’ve started to feel really sleepy.” Sunny said.

“Go on without me. I’ll just rest here a bit.”

Before George could say, sweet dreams, Sunny was sleeping soundly.

With a strong gust of wind came another voice. "Looks like you could use some help! I'm Windy. Allow me to show you around!"

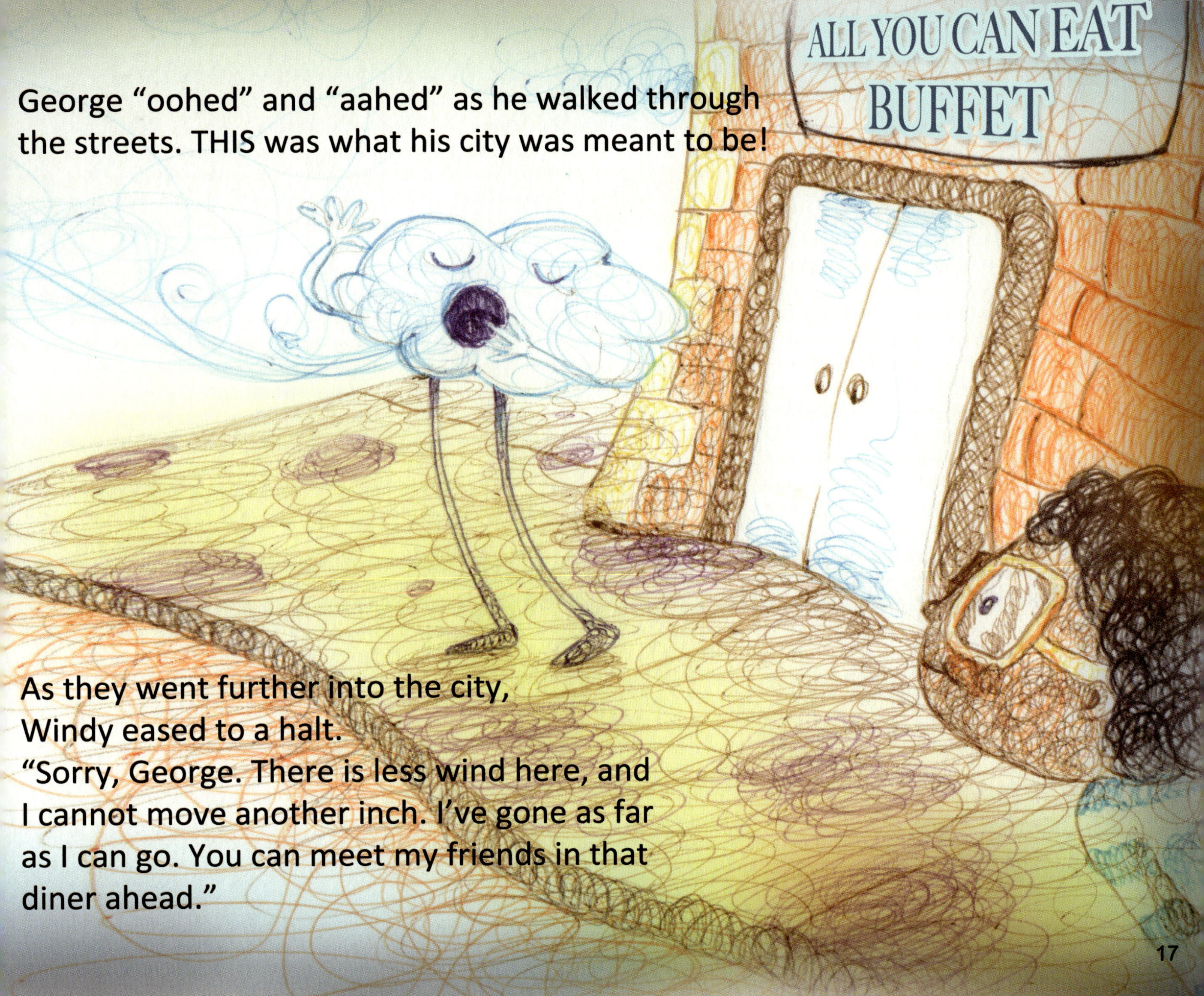

George "oohed" and "aahed" as he walked through the streets. THIS was what his city was meant to be!

As they went further into the city, Windy eased to a halt.
"Sorry, George. There is less wind here, and I cannot move another inch. I've gone as far as I can go. You can meet my friends in that diner ahead."

George pushed open the diner door and heard loud chomping coming from a nearby table.
He sat down. "My name is Coal!"
Coal said between bites.
"And I'm Gassy." Gassy burped before continuing his meal.

"Do you two also get tired?" George asked.
Coal shook his head and continued to eat.
Gassy replied, "No, we're always here whenever you need us!"
"Except if the buffet runs out!" Coal added.

"Mmmm," George said as he took the last bite of his dinner. He waited, but Gassy and Coal just kept eating and eating. Just as they finished one plate, another took its place.

‘Wow! You two must be hungry!”
George said.

“You betcha! We have to eat this much so we can work hard all the time,” replied Coal.

Tired of waiting, George said, “Goodbye!”

George wandered out of the city. In the distance, he saw a blue glow on the horizon.

As George approached, he saw an atom!
“Hi, I’m Nuke,” said the atom.
George asked, “Why are you all the way out here by yourself?”
“Well, people are a little scared of me. So, I work out here,” Nuke said.
“But I’m a really great neighbor!”

The sun set, and the wind stilled. The diner closed for the night.
"Even when my friends get hungry or sleepy,
I keep supplying energy to the city!"

Nuke started dancing
with his new friend.
George twirled round
and round ...

George woke up with a start as he
fell out of bed
"Eureka!" he yelled as he leapt up
from the floor.
"Cities can't work with just one form
of energy. It's best to have them all!"

George ran to find Marie.
“Marie! MARIE!” George shouted,
“I was wrong. We HAVE to work together! I tried,
but I can’t do it without you!”

George and Marie worked together to build a bigger, better city. “That’s wonderful, children! Your teamwork has empowered you and your city,” said Ms. Megawatt.

"The wind and sun provide
renewable energy,"
Ms. Megawatt continued.
"Coal and natural gas run
all the time no matter
the weather.
Nuclear is always
on providing clean energy.
Having diversity helped
achieve success!"

Glossary

Atoms: the tiny building blocks of matter
Chomping: to chew loudly and strongly
Circuit: a closed system especially of wires through which electricity can flow
Diversity: composed of different things
Empowered: to make stronger and more confident
Eureka: a cry of joy when one finds or discovers something
Exclaimed: to say something suddenly and loudly
Glee: great joy or happiness
Horizon: the line where the earth's surface and the sky appear to meet
Impatiently: restless or eager
Megawatt: a unit of energy (equal to 1,000,000 watts)
Twirled: spin quickly and repeatedly

Historical Figures

The characters in this story are named after important scientists in nuclear science history.

George Alcorn is a pioneering physicist and engineer noted for his aerospace and semiconductor inventions. He was inducted into the National Inventors Hall Fame for his x-ray imaging spectrometer. This device helps scientists better understand what materials are made of and has been used to search for new planets. George Alcorn also worked as an educator and promoted minorities in science, math, and engineering.

Marie Curie was a physicist and chemist who conducted research on radioactivity which is a term to describe elements that emit strong rays of energy. She was awarded a Nobel Prize in Physics and Chemistry for her work in radiation and discovery of the radioactive elements polonium and radium. During World War I, Marie learned that x-rays could help figure out what was wrong with injured soldiers. She realized putting the x-ray machines in trucks to move them around would allow all hospitals access to a machine.

The summer camp George and Marie attend is named after Thomas Edison who is credited with many inventions, including the electric light bulb, and holds over 1,000 US patents in his name.

If you enjoyed George's Energy Adventure, please checkout Marie's Electric Adventure! A story about George's camp friend, Marie, and her dog, Einstein, who head out on an adventure to turn the lights back on! Marie's Electric Adventure is available for free on iTunes.

Fun Energy Facts

Why is Nuke glowing blue? I thought something nuclear would be green slime!

The reason Nuke is glowing blue is because of Cherenkov radiation which is the characteristic underwater blue glow created in a nuclear reactor when a charged particle (such as an electron) passes through the water at a speed greater than the speed of light. There is no green slime produced at a nuclear plant. Fuel goes into the reactor as a solid and comes out as a solid.

Where did the characters from George's dream come from?

Sunny, Windy, Gassy, Coal, and Nuke are nicknames for the diverse energy sources used across the world to provide electricity. Sunny, or solar energy, is produced by converting the sun's rays to energy through the use of photovoltaic cells or solar cells. Windy, or wind energy, uses blades that are turned by the wind and attached to a generator which produces energy. Coal, or coal power plants, burn fossil fuels to produce heat which is converted to steam and turns a generator. Gassy, or natural gas, produces energy by combustion inside an engine, like in your parent's car, and is connected to a generator which produces electricity. Nuke, or nuclear energy, uses the energy from splitting atoms to produce steam and turn a generator.

How diverse is the energy sources used across the world?

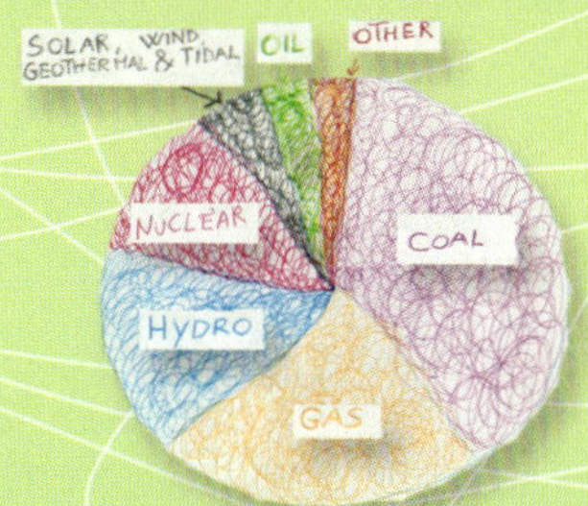

A focus on creating a diverse energy portfolio can reduce air pollution sure reliable energy. As of 2016, the world electricity production by source is 38.3% Coal, 23.1% gas, 16.6% hydro, 10.4% Nuclear, 5.6% solar/wind/geothermal/tidal, and 5% other. There is a need for new generating capacity around the world both to replace old fossil fuel units, which emit a lot of carbon dioxide, and to meet increased demand for electricity in many countries.

This book was funded by the North American Young Generation in Nuclear. The book project was organized and written by the following members of NAYGN: Matthew Bradfield, Kevin Burnett, Christine Johnsen, Amanda Lang, Glen Lawson, Nyria Maynard, Adam Reichenbach, Courtney Tampas, Jenny Taylor, and Natalie Wood

For more information about nuclear energy, check out the following resource:
https://naygn.org/committees/public-information/public-information-library

Published by
North American Young Generation in Nuclear (NAYGN)
P.O. Box 32642, Charlotte, NC 28232 USA
www.nagyn.org

Illustrated by
Kezia Terracciano
www.keziat.net

Manufactured in the United States.

978-0-578-21847-2